GREAT WESTERN REVIVAL

Hugh Ballantyne

First published in the United Kingdom in 1985 by
Jane's Publishing Company Limited
238 City Road, London EC1V 2PU

ISBN 0 7106 0337 1

Typeset by Netherwood Dalton & Co Ltd, Huddersfield

Printed by Netherwood Dalton & Co Ltd,
Huddersfield

Cover illustrations

Front: No 4930 *Hagley Hall*, beautifully maintained by the Severn
Valley Railway and sporting a Hawksworth tender, pulls away from
Pontypool Road with the 'Deeside Venturer'. 4 October 1980. (*Hugh
Ballantyne*)
Leica M4-2 50mm Summicron Kodachrome 25 1/500, f2-2.8

Rear: No 6000 *King George V* on the down slow line just entering
Sonning Cutting, east of Reading, with the special train run from
Paddington to Didcot to mark the 125th anniversary of the opening of
Paddington station. Sadly the 'King' ran hot at Didcot and the return
journey — much to the patrons' annoyance — was diesel-hauled. 1
March 1979. (*Hugh Ballantyne*)
Leica M3 50mm Summicron Kodachrome 25 1/250, f2

This page: Fireman's view from No 7812 *Erlestoke Manor* waiting for
the signal to proceed into Bridgnorth station on the Severn Valley
Railway. This was one of the original 20 'Manors' built by the GWR,
appearing from Swindon in 1939. Ten more were built by BR in 1950
and out of these 30 useful lightweight 4-6-0s no fewer than nine have
been preserved. Four (all featured in this book) are or have been in
active service since the period of our review. September 1979. (*D C
Williams*)
Pentax SP1000 55mm Takumar Kodachrome 64

Introduction

Those of us who recall the sense of grievous loss in 1968 when steam was finally eliminated by BR and then the feeling of despair by the succeeding unbending policy of BR absolutely to refuse any steam traction over its system (a few runs by A3 No 4472 and the narrow gauge Vale of Rheidol excepted) are still grateful to Sir Peter Prior of H P Bulmer Ltd. Backed by the many people in the railway preservation movement, in 1971 Sir Peter eventually persuaded BR senior management to relent and allow a limited return to steam for specials on selected routes.

It was wholly appropriate that *King George V*, the flag-bearer of the Great Western locomotive fleet, should be chosen to pioneer the way back. The Great Western had been the only railway company in the country to retain its corporate identity from its Act of Incorporation in 1835 right through to the last day of 1947 when the government of the day compulsorily nationalised this great institution and the three other major railway companies to form one large state-controlled system. Today we are indeed fortunate that due to the efforts of enthusiastic GWR preservationists, going back to the purchase of No 9017 in 1962 (well before the end of steam on the Western Region) so many fine GWR engines

and branch lines have not only been preserved but are back in operation or reopened in many parts of England to give us a permanent insight to what the Great Western was really like.

Having been born and brought up deep in GWR territory at Bath, I obviously have great affection for the Great Western. It was truly a great railway with an identity and character never equalled or surpassed by any other railway company. Therefore I particularly wish to thank the publishers for giving me this opportunity to put together a colourful reminder of most of the present active GW engines and the railways or centres on which they operate. This shows something of what has been achieved to keep the image of the company permanently alive. Likewise I sincerely thank my fellow photographers who have so kindly and willingly allowed me to use their valuable original transparencies.

HUGH BALLANTYNE
Eccleshall, North Staffordshire.
February 1985

Classic Great Western, very appropriately seen at the magnificent Great Western Society centre at Didcot. In front of the 1932-built shed (replacing an earlier structure) are Nos 5051 *Drysllwyn Castle*, in steam, 7808 *Cookham Manor*, 5900 *Hinderton Hall* and Churchward-designed Mogul No 5322. 29 July 1984. (*Hugh Ballantyne*)
Leica M4-2   50mm Summicron   Kodachrome 25   1/60, f5.6

At very short notice in the late summer of 1971, after a total BR steam ban for over three years, it was announced that *King George V* would haul four experimental excursions to assess the practical difficulties of operating steam-hauled trains over BR. Credit for negotiating this remarkable breakthrough is due to Mr Peter Prior, Group Managing Director of Hereford cider makers H P Bulmer Ltd, who had, at their expense, restored No 6000 to full working order. Here is the 'Return to Steam' special from Hereford to Tyseley, appropriately and fortuitously run on a lovely sunny early autumn day with *King George V*, at the head of the five Bulmers 'Cider Pullmans' and two BR seconds coming up the main line past the site of Magor station and heading towards the Severn Tunnel, Swindon and Oxford. 2 October 1971. (*Mrs Toni Ballantyne*) *Voigtlander CLR 50mm Skopar Agfa CT18 1/500, f2.8-4*

Left. The first GWR line to be reopened as a fully operational railway was the Dart Valley in South Devon running from Buckfastleigh to a point just outside Totnes station. Trains commenced running on 5 April 1969 with 0-6-0PT No 6412 marshalled in the middle of four coaches repainted in chocolate and cream livery in the manner seen above. This picture, taken during that first month, shows the train leaving Staverton and portrays the beautiful valley of the River Dart to best advantage in its lovely spring colours. April 1969. *(Peter W Gray)*
Pentax S1a 135mm Kodachrome II

Above. The Dart Valley also operates the only preserved Hawksworth 1600 class light 0-6-0PT. Seventy of these engines were built to GWR design in early BR days, the preserved example, No 1638, entering traffic in 1951. She is seen here heading down the branch near Dartington en route from Buckfastleigh to Totnes (Riverside). 12 June 1971. *(Leslie F Folkard)*
Agfa Silette 45mm Kodachrome II
1/200, f4

5

Above. The first standard gauge GWR locomotive bought for private preservation was 'Dukedog' 9000 class No 9017, which was purchased in running order from BR in March 1962 and sent to its new home on the Bluebell Railway in Sussex. There it has mainly operated with its original number 3217 and the name which was allocated but subsequently countermanded and never carried in service: *Earl of Berkeley*. It is seen in that condition outside the shed at Sheffield Park. Until the re-emergence of *City of Truro* in 1985 it had been the only outside-framed GWR engine in service and in 1984 was transferred to the GWS at Didcot in connection with the 1985 celebrations. 29 July 1983. (*Hugh Ballantyne*)
Leica M4-2   50mm Summicron
Kodachrome 25   1/60, f5.6

Right. A fine 1970 picture of the outside-framed 4-4-0 No 3217 *Earl of Berkeley* climbing the 1-75 gradient near Freshfield Halt, northbound from Sheffield Park towards Horsted Keynes. (*Michael Esau*)
Zeiss Super Ikonta   Agfa CT18   1/250, f5

Left. The GW served all the best cider apple-growing counties in England: Somerset, Devon and Herefordshire. The latter provides the backcloth for this scene of No 7808 *Cookham Manor* piloting No 6998 *Burton Agnes Hall* with the GWS vintage train on the last stages of their journey from Didcot to Hereford. The train is passing some of the orchards near the site of Stoke Edith station. 14 June 1975. (*T B Owen*)

Leica M2 50mm Summicron Kodachrome II 1/300, f3.2

Below. Numerically the second largest GWR tender engine class were the 'Halls', comprising 259 locomotives, or if you add the 71 'Modified Halls', a Hawksworth development of the earlier Collett series, 330 engines. All except the prototype No 4900 *Saint Martin* carried names of halls found not only on, but often miles away from GWR territory! The Great Western Society are the owners of two operational 'Halls', one of each series and here both are coupled together working a train on the demonstration line at Didcot. Collett series No 5900 *Hinderton Hall* (built 1931) is piloting Hawksworth 'Modified Hall' No 6998 *Burton Agnes Hall* (built 1949). 11 April 1977. (*T B Owen*)

Leica M2 50mm Summicron Kodachrome 64 1/500, f4.5

Prior to No 6000's ill-fated Paddington-Didcot run on 1 March 1979 commemorating 125 years of the GWR's London terminus, the 4-6-0 travelled under its own power from Swindon to Old Oak Common with the 6000 Locomotive Association van. This atmospheric study was taken at Old Oak on the evening of No 6000's arrival, 27 February. *(Hugh Dady)*
Praktica IV 50mm Tessar Ektachrome 64 5 secs, f4

The Paddington celebrations were also attended by 'Hall' No 5900 *Hinderton Hall* and 'Manor' No 7808 *Cookham Manor*. The pair travelled in steam from their GWS Didcot home early on 1 March together with two of the Society's vintage vehicles. Later that day *Hinderton Hall* is seen making use of the Old Oak Common turntable in preparation for its journey home. (*Hugh Dady*)

Praktica IV   50mm Tessar   Ektachrome 64 5 secs, f4.5

11

Opposite. On one of the shortest days of the year the pink rays of the setting sun reflect on the exhaust of 0-6-0PT No 5764 as she heads towards Northwood with the last train of the day, the 3.00 pm from Bewdley to Arley. 28 December 1976. *(Hugh Ballantyne) Leica M3 50mm Summicron Kodachrome 25 1/250, f2.8*

Left. On a fine and warm early spring afternoon during the SVR's Spring Gala Weekend, Collett-designed 5101 class 2-6-2T No 5164 sets out across Bewdley south viaduct with the 1.15 pm train from Bridgnorth to Foley Park. The big Prairie had returned to service after restoration just four months previously. 12 April 1980. *(Hugh Ballantyne) Leica M3 50mm f2 Summicron Kodachrome 25 1/500, f2/2.8*

Since the 'Return to Steam' there have been two major events commemorating important 150-year railway anniversaries. The first was the 'Rail 150' exhibition to celebrate the opening of the Stockton and Darlington Railway in 1825 at Shildon, its highlight being the cavalcade of steam locomotives to Heighington. The caval- cade only took place once and three GWR engines participated in the proceedings: No 6960 *Raveningham Hall* from the Severn Valley Railway, No 7808 *Cookham Manor* from the GWS at Didcot and 0-6-0PT No 7752 from Birmingham Railway Museum, Tyseley. Here the pannier tank sets out from Shildon against the unfamiliar surroundings of County Durham and the NER signal box as the ninth participant of 35 featured in the cavalcade. 31 August 1975. (*Peter J C Skelton*)
Canon FTb 50mm Kodachrome II 1/250, f4-5.6

The year 1980 witnessed 'Rocket 150', staged at Rainhill on the Liverpool & Manchester line to commemorate 150 years since the opening of the Liverpool & Manchester Railway, the first public steam-hauled passenger railway in the world. This too had a cavalcade of locomotives and rolling stock but was billed to have 40 particip- ants and took place on the three days of the Spring Bank Holiday weekend. Again three GWR engines took part, two under their own steam, 0-6-0 No 3205 from the Severn Valley Railway, seen above as sixteenth in the proces- sion, and Didcot's No 5051 *Drysllwyn Castle*. The third engine was the 2ft 6in gauge 0-6-0T *The Earl* from the Welshpool & Llanfair Light Railway, conveyed on a weltrol wagon in a train hauled by LMS Class 5 No 5000. 24 May 1980.

(Hugh Ballantyne)
Leica M3   90mm   Kodachrome 25

Above. No 3205 is the only preserved member of Mr Collett's 2251 class, of which 120 were constructed between 1930 and 1948. This engine was built in 1946 and withdrawn only 19 years later, so it has been preserved longer than it was in revenue service, as is the case with many engines. Initially restored at Buckfastleigh in 1966, she came to Bridgnorth in 1967, and when the first part of the preserved Severn Valley Railway opened to Hampton Loade on 23 May 1970, No 3205 hauled the first public passenger train. This engine remains very active and is seen here looking quite immaculate at Highley on a Spring Gala Day with a goods train to Bewdley. 25 April 1982. *(Hugh Ballantyne)* *Leica M4-2 50mm Summicron Kodachrome 25 1/60, f4-5.6*

Right. The first 'Manor' to arrive on the SVR was No 7819 *Hinton Manor*, which had seen a lot of service on the Cambrian section, including Royal Train duty with No 7822 in 1963. This locomotive came from the Barry scrapyard in 1973 and after four years of painstaking work, entered regular SVR service in the late summer of 1977. This picture shows No 7819 in pristine condition just back into traffic 12 years after withdrawal by BR, heading a Bewdley train near Oldbury viaduct, south of Bridgnorth. 2 October 1977. *(Hugh Ballantyne)* *Leica M3 50mm Summicron Kodachrome 25 1/500, f2-2.8*

Left. No 1363 was one of five 0-6-0ST 1361 class engines designed by Mr Churchward and built in 1910. They were all withdrawn in 1961/62 but fortunately this locomotive was sold for preservation, first going to Totnes in 1964, then to the GWS group at Bodmin who, with commendable effort restored it to running order in 1970. Steamings were held at Bodmin and this picture shows such an event with this attractive little engine and train running towards Bodmin General station. Unfortunately GWS operations at Bodmin were curtailed and No 1363 was transferred to 'headquarters' at Didcot, where she can now be seen. 22 July 1972. (*Peter W Gray*) *Pentax S1a 55mm Super Takumar Kodachrome 25*

Above. Another small GWR tank engine much admired is the distinctive Collett 1400 class 0-4-2T fitted for push-pull auto-train working. Four of the class of 75 engines have been preserved, Nos 1420 and 1450 on the Dart Valley, No 1442 also in Devon on static display at Tiverton Museum and this one, No 1466, active, like its Dart Valley sisters, at Didcot. This picture shows her shunting at the GWS centre flanked by the museum and buffet complex on the left and the diminutive Wantage Tramway 0-4-0WT No 5 on the right. 29 July 1984. (*Hugh Ballantyne*) *Leica M4-2 50mm Summicron Kodachrome 25 1/125, f4*

19

Left. On a bright spring day No 5051 *Drysllwyn Castle* gets into her stride as she climbs the 1 in 92 gradient around the south side of Hereford after taking over a southbound 'Welsh Marches Pullman' for the run down to Newport. 16 April 1983. (*Hugh Ballantyne*)
Leica M4-2   90mm Summicron   Kodachrome 25

1/500, f2.8

Above. GWR preservation at its zenith! Nos 7808 *Cookham Manor* and 6998 *Burton Agnes Hall* lead the GWS vintage train through the Malverns east of Ledbury tunnel on 14 June 1975, returning from Hereford to Didcot. Sadly

the high cost of meeting BR's maintenance and inspection requirements for privately owned vehicles now confines this magnificent set of period carriages to the GWS Didcot depot. (*L A Nixon*)
Nikon F   85mm Nikkor   Kodachrome II   1/500, f2.8

Right. Two more GWS-owned and Didcot-based engines enjoying a running-in turn on the main line to Oxford and back, 2-6-2T No 6106 piloting No 6998 *Burton Agnes Hall* with a three-coach train at Hinksey, south of Oxford. No 6106 is the only example of the 70 Collett-designed 6100 class to be preserved. 1 July 1973. *(T B Owen)*
Leica M2 50mm Summicron Kodachrome II 1/300, f3.2

Opposite. 'Modified Hall' No 6998 *Burton Agnes Hall* makes a fine sight at the head of a GWS special from Didcot to Hereford running over a section of bullhead track near Malvern en route to Hereford. This engine was BR-built in January 1949, withdrawn in December 1965 and sold to the GWS for preservation in 1966. 24 June 1973. *(T B Owen)*
Leica M2 50mm Summicron Kodachrome II 1/300, f3.2

Left. Another attractive preserved line, and one uni[c] in that it was the only section railway so far taken over by preservation company direc[t] from BR without having fir[st] been closed to traffic, is the Torbay and Dartmouth Railway, which runs from Paignton to Kingswear in So[uth] Devon. Skirting the River D[art] at the southern end of the railway, small Prairie tank N[o] 4588 with a good load of se[ven] coaches has just started the climb up to Churston to be followed by the downhill run [to] Paignton. 27 May 1975. (*L A Nixon*)
Leica M3   50mm Summilux Kodachrome II   1/250, f4

Right. Besides the run down[n] into Kingswear, beautifully situated on the east side of t[he] River Dart estuary overlooki[ng] Dartmouth, the Torbay and Dartmouth Railway provides good views over the sparklin[g] blue waters of Torbay and across to Berry Head. This picture shows the attractive seascape behind No 7827 *Lydham Manor* climbing the 1 [in] 60 gradient at Broadsands on [a] warm summer day with a Kingswear-bound train. 24 August 1974. (*Leslie F Folkar[d]*
Agfa Silette   45mm Kodachrome II   1/200, f4

Right. Large and powerful 2-8-0T No 5239, one of Mr Collett's 5205 class of heavy mineral engines, has been restored and provides plenty of muscle for hauling trains on the steeply graded Torbay and Dartmouth Railway. This engine was bought from Barry in 1973 having been withdrawn by BR in December 1963. Since restoration it has been painted in GWR unlined green livery and given the name *Goliath*. It is seen in this condition climbing from Goodrington towards Churston with a train to Kingswear. 14 July 1981. *(Peter J C Skelton)*
Hasselblad 500CM
80mm lens
Ektachrome 64   1/500, f4

Opposite. Another smart Torbay and Dartmouth Railway train of GWR chocolate and cream-liveried (but mainly BR-built) coaches, hauled by 4500 class 2-6-2T No 4555, leaves Paignton for Kingswear. 16 July 1981. *(Peter J C Skelton)*
Hasselblad 500CM
80mm lens
Ektachrome 64   1/500, f4

Left. The small Prairie tanks of typical and distinctive GWR appearance are popular engines for preservation on lines wanting GWR representation due to their wide route availability and economical operating size. There are three of the original 4500 class Churchward series preserved and the SVR's example, No 4566, has put in much useful work on that line. Backlit by the autumn sun on the approach to Eardington, No 4566 has just come off the Sterns permanent way slack hauling a train of stock in the early BR passenger livery from Bewdley to Bridgnorth. 2 October 1977. (*Hugh Ballantyne*)
Leica M3 50mm Summicron Kodachrome 25

Above. The preserved lines in this country now not only pride themselves on the restoration achievements carried out to locomotives and rolling stock, but also maintain their stations to a much better standard than ever contemplated by their previous owner, thus recalling the part played by rural stations in bygone days. Arley, on the SVR, is such a station and, blessed with a lovely location on the west side of the River Severn, is understandably popular with visitors to the railway and the adjoining countryside. It also won the award of Best Kept Preserved Station in the competition held in 1983. On the first day of the 1976 season No 4566 is arriving at Arley with a short train from Highley to Bewdley. 6 March 1976. (*Hugh Ballantyne*)
Leica M3 50mm Summicron Kodachrome 25
1/125, f2.8

In 1964 well known 'Castle' No 4079 *Pendennis Castle* was withdrawn and sold in working order for preservation. It was the seventh of the class to be constructed in February 1924 and achieved fame by taking part in a locomotive exchange with LNER Pacific No 4474 (later named *Victor Wild*) in 1925, proving to the LNER authorities the sound basis upon which Collett had designed the lighter 4-6-0. No 4079 was passed for running on BR lines in the 1970s and the immaculate engine is seen at speed approaching Dorrington signal box, between Shrewsbury and Hereford, hauling a returning special to Northampton. 6 April 1974. (*Hugh Ballantyne*) *Leica M3   50mm Summicron   Kodachrome II 1/500, f2-2.8*

In 1977 the owner of *Pendennis Castle* announced that his locomotive was being sold to Hammersley Iron Pty Ltd in Western Australia. After an overhaul at Carnforth prior to departure, this lovely engine made a farewell run from Tyseley to Didcot and back. The train was titled the 'Great Western Envoy' and is seen on the climb from Leamington approaching the short Harbury tunnel on the outward run. Six days later she left her native land, sentenced to transportation to Dampier, on the remote north western coast of Western Australia and about as far away as it is possible to find a railway. Note the red Hammersley Iron emblems painted on the centre splasher and placed below the coat of arms on the tender. 29 May 1977. *(T B Owen) Leica M2 50mm Summicron Kodachrome 64 1/125, f2.8*

Left. The king of kings, No 6000 *King George V*, leaving his home base of Hereford and just getting into his stride up grade towards Shelwick Junction en route to Chester with the 'Deeside Venturer'. 4 October 1980. (*Hugh Ballantyne*) *Leica M4-2 50mm Summicron Kodachrome 25*

Right. The 'Midland Jubilee' tour gave patrons haulage by four engines, one from each grouped company, starting from Shrewsbury to Chester with LNER *Sir Nigel Gresley*, back to Shrewsbury with LMS *Princess Elizabeth* and with *King George V* for the short section to Craven Arms. The train was photographed just over a mile to the north of this rural junction. For the last leg from Craven Arms to Newport, SR *Clan Line* completed the quartet of steam. 1 October 1977. (*Hugh Ballantyne*) *Leica M3 135mm Kodachrome 25 1/500, f2.8*

Fifteen of Collett's 842 ubiquitous 5700 class 0-6-0PTs have been preserved. Six of these came from London Transport, who had bought surplus BR stock during the late 1950s and early 1960s. The most northerly resident of the fifteen survivors is No 5775, which was purchased by the Keighley and Worth Valley Railway from London Transport in January 1970. Whilst in London the Panniers were painted in the attractive LT red livery lined black and yellow, and this interesting photograph shows the 0-6-0PT as LT No L89 coming off shed at Haworth, two months after arrival in Yorkshire. 30 March 1970. (L A Nixon)

Leica M3 50mm Summilux Kodachrome II

This picture should be compared with that opposite and shows what a difference a coat of paint can make to an engine. Here, the same engine, KWVR Pannier tank L89, is standing in Haworth loco yard painted in a light brown livery applied for filming purposes but which it sported for some years. The engine retained its LT number. For 5700 class engines in GWR livery see pages 14, 38, 39 and 40. 28 August 1973. *(Hugh Ballantyne)*
Leica M3 50mm Summicron Kodachrome II 1/60, f5.6

Above. Finished in BR lined green livery (which was only a slight variation on GWR livery), No 7812 *Erlestoke Manor* looks good in the late winter sunshine accelerating uphill towards Hay Bridge after the Sterns permanent way slack with the 2.45 pm train from Bewdley to Bridgnorth. 13 March 1982. (*Hugh Ballantyne*)
Leica M4-2   50mm Summicron   Kodachrome 25 1/500, f2/2.8

Right. Although there are eight of the 5101 class large Prairies saved from extinction, at present only one of the Severn Valley Railway's stock of three and none of the others is operational. No 5164, built in October 1930, worked in the Midlands until 1957 when she went to Newton Abbot until withdrawal in April 1963. The engine was purchased from Woodhams, Barry, in 1972 and arrived in company with sisters Nos 4141, 4930 *Hagley Hall* and 7819 *Hinton Manor*

at Bewdley in January 1973. After major overhaul she returned to traffic in December 1979 and has become a very active member of the SVR fleet. This picture shows her crossing Victoria Bridge with the 2.30 pm from Bridgnorth to Bewdley on a lovely summer day a few weeks before the extension to Kidderminster was opened. 8 July 1984. (*Hugh Ballantyne*)
Leica M4-2   50mm Summicron   Kodachrome 25 1/250, f2.8

Left. The handsome nameplates evolved for GWR locomotives formed an essential element of the character of these machines. The three examples depicted here were taken in the early days of GW preservation and need no further introduction.

Above. The bell borne by No 6000 *King George V* was presented by the Baltimore and Ohio Railroad to mark the locomotive's outstandingly successful visit to the USA in the autumn of 1927, and carries a suitably appropriate inscription. (all: *Hugh Ballantyne*)
Voigtlander CLR 50mm Skopar Agfa CT18

Opposite. Churchward Mogul No 5322 was the first GWR engine saved from Woodhams scrapyard at Barry in 1969, when it made the short journey to Caerphilly for restoration. It is one of only two of the 342 4300 class Moguls preserved; the other, No 9303, is undergoing long-term restoration on the Severn Valley Railway. This engine was subsequently transferred to Didcot and although steamed in the early 1970s it is not currently in running order. However, as can be seen, its external appearance is very good. This picture shows her posed alongside the coal stage at Didcot on 29 July 1984. (*Hugh Ballantyne*)
Leica M4-2 50mm Summicron Kodachrome 25 1/60, f5.6

Left. At present the Quainton Railway Society at Quainton Road station, north west of Aylesbury, only have this representative of the GWR amongst their working engines, although they are host to Sentinel No 12, No 6024 *King Edward I*, No 6989 *Wightwick Hall*, No 7200 and No 9466. 5700 class 0-6-0PT No 7715, built by Kerr Stuart in 1930, was another example sold by BR to LT in 1963 to become their No L99. Purchased by the Quainton Society in 1970, it has since reverted to GWR livery but is seen here in early BR black on a steam day on 28 August 1972. (*T B Owen*)
Leica M2 50mm Summicron Kodachrome II 1/250, f3.2

Right. Another centre of GWR flavour making progress in the long, hard uphill preservation battle is the Dean Forest Railway, based north of Lydney at Norchard, in the Forest of Dean. Negotiations still continue with BR for the acquisition of four miles of the former Severn and Wye Joint line in the Forest, but at Norchard, seen here, there is much activity. Restored small Prairie No 5541 in unlined green livery makes a pleasing sight passing 0-6-0PT No 9681. The latter was not operational when the picture was taken but came back into service at the end of September 1984. August 1984. (*Peter J C Skelton*)
Hasselblad 2000FC 80mm lens Ektachrome 64 1/125, f5.6

Left. With commendable resolution the Worcester Locomotive Society in 1969 bought one of the London Transport 0-6-0PTs, No L92, and set about restoring it as GWR No 5786. Initially preserved at Bridgnorth it was later transferred to the Bulmers Railway Centre at Hereford, where a small band of devoted enthusiasts have painstakingly restored the locomotive and maintain it in working order. This picture shows her during a Bulmers open day resplendent in GWR livery (but still awaiting transfer numbers on the buffer beam). 26 May 1974. (*D R G Nowell*)
Practika L 50mm Zeiss Agfa CT18 1/250, f4

Right. Spectacular sight of the SVR's 'Hall' No 4930 *Hagley Hall* enjoying to the full one of its main line outings pounding up Llanvihangel bank with a 'Welsh Marches Pullman' heading for Newport. 19 February 1983. *(Peter J C Skelton)*
Yashica FR1   135mm lens
Kodachrome 25   1/250, f3.5

Opposite. Visual evidence of the result of hard work and a wonderful success story is apparent in this splendid picture of No 4930 *Hagley Hall* piloting LMS No 5000 on the 'Inter City' tour, seen making a fast run towards Rossett to gain speed for the immediate climb ahead up the 1 in 82 of Gresford bank, north of Wrexham. This was the first service run of No 4930 and it is remarkable that this immaculate engine had been withdrawn by BR in November 1963, sold to Woodham Bros for scrap in 1964 to languish at Barry for eight years before purchase by the SVR in 1972. Then followed another seven years of renovation and the result — and reward — is seen here with the engine now in regular service on the SVR and enjoying runs on BR-approved lines from time to time. 22 September 1979. *(Peter J C Skelton)*
Hasselblad 500CM   80mm lens
Ektachrome 64   1/500, f4

Left. Paradoxically the longest preserved line in the country, the West Somerset Railway, which runs for 22¾ miles from Minehead to Bishops Lydeard, only has three GWR tank locomotives in its stock list. Two of these are small Prairie tanks under repair and the third is 6400 class 0-6-0PT No 6412 which was transferred from the Dart Valley Railway in 1976. The line traverses pleasant coastal and pastoral countryside and this picture shows No 6412 in a typical Somerset setting of lush green farmland near Williton, the principle intermediate station on the railway. 22 October 1977. (*T B Owen*) *Leica M2 50mm Summicron Kodachrome 64 1/250, f3.2*

Above. In Shropshire a short section of the GW branch between Wellington and Buildwas at Horsehay is the home of the Horsehay Steam Trust. By 1980 this group had restored in unlined green livery Collett 5600 class 0-6-2T No 5619, which was saved from Barry in May 1973, and in 1984 she went into passenger service hauling their train on steaming weekends, usually the last Sunday in each month. Although eight of the 200 5600 class are preserved, and Didcot's No 6697 was a very early preserved locomotive to be put back into steam, Horsehay's engine was the only class member at work in 1984. This picture shows the train at Horsehay on 26 August 1984. (*Hugh Ballantyne*) *Leica M4-2 50mm Summicron Kodachrome 25 1/125, f4*

Above. Express passenger engine running on a main line, thanks to the cooperation of BR in allowing selected preserved locomotives to run on specified sections of the national network. This picture shows Didcot's No 5051 *Drysllwyn Castle* just north of Aynho Junction on the former GWR main line to Birmingham, crossing the River Cherwell, which at this point forms the county boundary between Oxford and Northampton, with a Didcot to Stratford on Avon special one sunny spring morning. 14 April 1984. *(Hugh Ballantyne)*
Leica M4-2   90mm Summicron   Kodachrome 25   1/500, f2

Right. A main line run with a difference, but still a fine sight. 4-6-0 No 7808 *Cookham Manor* is hauling a train of GWS stock through Chesterfield, very much on Midland Railway territory in Derbyshire, heading home to Didcot after taking part in the exhibition (and the engine in the cavalcade) at the Rail 150 celebrations, Shildon, County Durham. The vehicle next to the tender is a 1937-built 'Siphon G', No 2796, one of the GWR's bogie general purpose vans once familiar in service all over the system. 1 September 1975. *(L A Nixon)*
Nikon F   85mm Nikkor   Kodachrome II   1/250, f4

The first 2-8-0 type in Great Britain, later to become a very popular wheel arrangement for goods engines, was Churchward's 2800 class, introduced with a prototype, No 97, way back in 1903 and subsequently extended to a class of 84 by 1919. A modified series, the 2884 class, totalling 83 locomotives was constructed between 1938 and 1942. Six are preserved, and the SVR's example, No 2857, did a little steaming in 1979/80. It is seen here one sunny evening catching the low sunlight at Bewdley during a filming sequence for the BBC's 'God's Wonderful Railway'. In the meantime, at the GWS Didcot depot work is proceeding well and it is expected their 2884 class, No 3822, will be back in service in 1985. 19 July 1980. *(Peter J C Skelton) Contax RTS 50mm Kodachrome 25 1/500, f2*

The SVR also have use of another 'Hall' class engine on their railway, this being the second built of the Hawksworth 'Modified Hall' 6959 class, No 6960 *Raveningham Hall*, introduced in 1944. It was withdrawn by BR in 1964, went the familiar way to Woodhams scrapyard at Barry, and was saved and sent to Carnforth for restoration in 1972. This was achieved by 1975, when it took part in the Rail 150 celebrations at Shildon. In 1977 it was transferred to the SVR and is seen here leaving Bewdley with the 12.05 pm train from Bridgnorth to Foley Park during the spring 1980 enthusiasts' weekend. 12 April 1980. *(Hugh Ballantyne)*
Leica M3   50mm Summicron   Kodachrome 25 1/500, f2/2.8

Left. This picture reminds us that on so many occasions indifferent light and thick cloud play a major role in the weather pattern over the British Isles, but for all that, there is atmosphere and drama in this study of No 5051 *Drysllwyn Castle* storming out of Oxford on a murky January day with 'The Phoenix', run from Didcot to Stratford on Avon hauling the GWS vintage stock to celebrate the return to service of this elegant express passenger engine. 19 January 1980. *(T B Owen)*
Leica M2 90mm Summicron Kodachrome 64 1/125, f3.2

Above. Further north the photographer had the benefit of high pressure thus giving cloudless skies and — in winter — low temperatures, ingredients which he has put to excellent use with this striking picture emphasising the billowing exhaust of Nọ 5051 *Drysllwyn Castle* at Claverdon, returning from Stratford on Avon over the single line section between Bearley Junction and Hatton. 19 January 1980. *(T B Owen)*
Leica M2 50mm Summicron Kodachrome 25 1/300, f3.2

King class No 6000 *King George V*, the flagship of the GWR fleet and, as the most powerful 4-6-0 type built in this country, Mr Collett's masterpiece, heads westbound on the down fast at Undy, near Severn Tunnel Junction with the 'Brunel Pullman', en route from Bristol Temple Meads to Hereford via Newport. 12 June 1983. (*Hugh Ballantyne*)

Leica M4-2   90mm Summicron   Kodachrome 25   1/500, f2

The last 'Castle' in service with BR was No 7029 *Clun Castle*, one of the series built after nationalisation in May 1950. Officially it was withdrawn from service in December 1965 although its last BR job was to haul the 17.00 Gloucester to Cheltenham train on 1 January 1966, so giving it the dubious honour of making the last regular service steam working on the former Great Western Railway. It was then sold in working order to Mr P B Whitehouse and has remained based at the Standard Gauge Steam Trust, Tyseley, Birmingham ever since. From time to time it makes main line runs and Gresford bank provides the setting for this broadside which clearly portrays the locomotive's double chimney. On 7 October 1978 *Clun Castle* was in charge of a 'Marches Venturer' working. (*Peter J C Skelton*)
Hasselblad 500cm 80mm
Agfa CT18 1/500, f4

Left. A representative engine from one of the smallest Welsh railways, No 813 was absorbed into the Great Western at the time of the Grouping on 1 January 1923. This little 0-6-0ST was one of 22 engines acquired with the assets of the Port Talbot Railway & Docks, being their No 26. It was built by Hudswell Clark in 1900 and sold by the GWR in January 1934 to Backworth Colliery Ltd in Northumberland. Eventually on nationalisation of the coal industry in 1947 it vested in the NCB and sold to an enthusiast, Mr P H Goss, in 1967. Although it has only steamed a nominal mileage on the SVR it was taken as a static exhibit to Rail 150 Shildon in 1975 and, as seen here at Bewdley, has been kept in good external condition for public display. 19 Sep-

tember 1976. (*D C Williams*)
Pentax SP1000   55mm Super Takumar
Kodachrome 64   1/100, f6.3

Above. The GWR was a pioneer in the utilisation of diesel railcars. After experiments with an AEC single-engined vehicle in 1933 around the Reading area, this first machine was put into service in February 1934 and during that year three more were built, all with two engines. The bodywork was by Park Royal Coachwork Ltd and bore a pleasing streamlined style. By 1937 a total of 18 had been built, of which one, No 17, was a parcels-only railcar. Another batch of 20, but this time with bodies constructed at Swin-

don, were built between 1940 and 1942, and again one of these, No 34, was a parcels car. The later series did not have quite the same rounded streamlined form although they show flair and originality in their appearance, which is more than can be said for the next generation of DMUs which appeared on BR twenty years later. However, you may judge for yourself by looking at this interesting picture at Didcot, which shows No 4 (built 1934) on the left (now in Swindon Railway Museum) and No 22 (built 1940) and owned by the GWS. 25 November 1978. (*Peter W Gray*)
Pentax S1a   55mm Super Takumar
Kodachrome 25

Left. Spring in Devon on the Dart Valley Railway and a beautiful setting for 0-4-2T No 1450 *Ashburton* crossing the River Dart near Buckfastleigh with a train to Totnes (Riverside). 3 April 1983. (*Michael Esau*)
Rolleiflex 3.5f
Agfa CT18   1/250, f4

Right. An interesting temporary loan took place in the summer of 1984 with the GWS 0-4-2T No 1466 going from Didcot to a new pasture deep in South East England as a visitor to the Kent and East Sussex Railway. This picture shows the little GWR engine in pleasant surroundings coming up Tenterden bank with a goods train from Rolvenden. 3 June 1984. (*Michael Esau*)

The GWR acquired three narrow gauge railways, all of different gauge, two of which came into the fold as part of the assets of the Cambrian Railways on 1 January 1923. Both of these little lines survived with the engines operating on them at the time of nationalisation in 1948, but the 2 ft 3 in gauge Corris Railway acquired in 1930, and which ran northwards from Machynlleth to Aberllefeni, was closed in August 1948 after flooding of the River Dovey eroded an embankment, making the railway bridge over it unsafe. The two Corris engines, Nos 3 and 4, were sold by BR in March 1951 to the Talyllyn Railway, the first preservation railway in the country, and have remained there in service ever since. Both have retained their Corris numbers and here 0-4-2ST No 3 *Sir Haydn* (temporarily painted red and renamed *Sir Handel*), built by Falcon Engineering in 1878, leaves Towyn Pendre with the 12.25 pm from Wharf station to Nant Gwernol. 21 June 1982. *(Hugh Ballantyne)* *Leica M4-2 90mm Summicron Kodachrome 25 1/250, f2.8/4*

The other Corris Railway engine was also an 0-4-2ST, numbered 4 and built by Kerr Stuart in 1921. This picture shows it in the dark green livery lined black and yellow of the Talyllyn Railway, who have also named it *Edward Thomas*, approaching Brynglas with the 11.00 am train from Towyn Wharf to Nant Gwernol. 31 August 1981. (*Hugh Ballantyne*)
Leica M4-2 50mm Summicron Kodachrome 25

Above. It is well known that the three 1 ft 11½ in gauge 2-6-2Ts working on the Vale of Rheidol line from Aberystwyth to Devils Bridge are the only steam locomotives now operated by BR. Two of them, Nos 7 and 8, were built by the GWR at Swindon in July 1923 whilst the third, No 9, is the survivor of the original pair built by Davies and Metcalfe of Manchester in 1902. BR named all three in 1956 and in the late 1960s they were painted in the corporate, all-pervading blue livery of the national system. This picture shows No 9 *Prince of Wales* and train in that blue livery crossing the timber bridge over the River Rheidol at Llanbadarn, heading eastwards towards Devils Bridge. 24 July 1969. (*L A Nixon*)

Leica M3   50mm Summilux   Kodachrome II 1/250, f3.5

Right. Now repainted in an early Vale of Rheidol yellow ochre livery, No 9 *Prince of Wales* looks quite different to its picture opposite, and certainly stands out well against the densely wooded background as he nears the end of the climb from Capel Bangor to the terminus at Devils Bridge. 19 June 1983. (*Hugh Ballantyne*)

Leica M4-2   50mm Summicron   Kodachrome 25 1/500, f2.8

The most easterly of the three narrow gauge lines is the Welshpool & Llanfair Light Railway which also has the widest track gauge, 2 ft 6 in for its eight miles between the two places which give it its name. The railway was opened in 1903 and started adjacent to the standard gauge station in Welshpool, one mile longer than now operated. From the start it had two 0-6-0Ts built by Beyer Peacock and they operated the entire service until passenger trains stopped in 1931 and BR finally closed the whole railway to goods traffic in 1956. A fine effort by a small, enthusiastic society secured this delightful railway for posterity in 1963 and both the little engines remain on the line, although in recent years neither have been available for traffic. *The Earl* (ex-GWR No 822) has been on loan to the NRM York for exhibition and *The Countess* (ex-GWR No 823 *Countess*) has been under repair at Llanfair. In earlier times *The Countess* is seen here leaving Castle Caerinion with the 4.35 pm train to Llanfair. 3 June 1969. (*Hugh Ballantyne*)
Voigtlander CLR 50mm Skopar
Agfa CT18 1/250, f5.6-8

This picture shows 0-6-0T No 1 *The Earl* leaving Sylfaen, then the eastern operational end of the line, with a train to Llanfair, whilst on the right 0-6-2T No 12 *Joan* (built by Kerr Stuart in 1927) is on running-in trials after restoration pending entry into service. 8 April 1977. (*Hugh Ballantyne*)

Leica M3   50mm Summicron   Kodachrome 25
1/125, f3·5

To qualify for inclusion in this book every engine illustrated has been in steam, however briefly, since the 'Return to Steam' by BR in October 1971 except this one. Still, what true Great Western enthusiast could refuse to look at such a magnificent locomotive epitomising the unsurpassed quality of Swindon products, even those dating so far back in history as this one which was built in May 1903? It is with eager anticipation that all GWR devotees await the return to service of *City of Truro* in 1985. Not only is she the record-holder with what is reasonably thought to be the first 'hundred', 102.3mph down from Whiteball tunnel in 1904, but when the unbelievable happened and No 3717 emerged from Swindon Museum on 10 July 1984 this was the *second* time this locomotive was removed from a museum for return to service! In the early hours of 14 July 1984 she was stealthily towed by No 37304 from Swindon to Kidderminster and Bewdley, then placed in the safe custody of the SVR where our photographer was fortunately on hand to get this unique picture of No 3717 pausing at Arley en route to Bridgnorth, with her towing partner 0-6-0 No 3205 discreetly and briefly backed away whilst the photograph was made. 14 July 1984. (*John Kenward*)

Canon AE-1 Program   Tamron SP 35-80mm Ektachrome 200